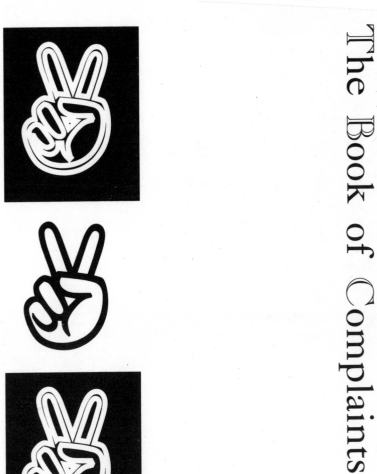

The Book of Complaints

Books by Richard Katrovas

Green Dragons (1983)
Snug Harbor (1986)
The Public Mirror (1990)
The Book of Complaints (1993)

The Book of Complaints

Richard Katrovas

8/11/93
—For a sweetheart,
of a student,
—I'll never forget
that day
you were
so happy

CARNEGIE MELLON UNIVERSITY PRESS PITTSBURGH 1993

Acknowledgments

Poems from *The Book of Complaints* first appeared in:
>Crazyhorse
>Denver Quarterly
>North American Review
>New Virginia Review
>Negative Capability
>and
>Southern Review.

I am grateful to Georgene Lovecky for assisting me in garnering additional Fulbright funding in the autumn of 1989, and I am grateful to the University of New Orleans for summer research grants. I must also thank my colleague and friend Mary Fitsgerald for wise criticism, and my friend the poet Peter Cooley for the same. Finally, I thank the editors of *Crazyhorse* for giving me their Poetry Award for 1991.

Publication of this book is supported by grants from the National Endowment for the Arts in Washington D.C., a Federal agency, and from the Pennsylvania Council for the Arts.

Contents

This Book is Ema's.

I

He will yet fill your mouth with laughter,
and shouts of joy will be on your lips;
your enemies shall be wrapped in confusion,
and the tents of the wicked shall vanish away.

Job 8, 21-24

Author's note:
Diacritics have been omitted from Czech words. Please read *ch* for *c* in Dubcek, Obcansky, and Kyticka; and *sh* for *s* in Svejk, Smid, Srut, Stepan, and Jakes. Distinctions between long and short syllables are lost on most non-speakers of Czech.

The Bridge of Intellectuals

If Crane had been a Czech, and deigned to live
till '53, he might have more than praised
a bridge, for in that year of Stalin's death,
artists and intellectuals of Prague—
but only those the Party had to fix
after an "elegant coup" in '48—
finished their bridge across the Vltava.

Each morning did they bring their lunch in bags?
Did they bitch and curse and clown around behind
the foremen's backs? Were there foremen? Or did
each man (were there women?) pull his weight
unprodded by the ethos of his class?
Of eleven bridges down the spine of Prague
it stands the shabbiest and least necessary.
From the road leaving town one sees the tufts
of grass and weeds muscling through the rusted
transoms that trains, some say, must rarely cross,
and notes the webbed faults in the dark concrete
of columns lifting from the water like
wet khaki pantlegs of old fishermen.
To those whose ambitions for bourgeois fame
got them torn from their tasks to labor here,
is there ironic consolation that,
as work is a matter of identity,
so many praised workers remain unnamed?

Anonymous bones of generations lie
the snaking length of China's ancient shyness;
unknown apprentices applied the strokes
that smeared celestial radiance onto cheeks
of lesser angels in the master works.
Such petty, silly little men, who snapped
the blossom of a generation from
its living vine, have watched their own bridge crumble,
and even as this bad joke stands unused,
dilapidated on the edge of town,
perhaps its "rehabilitated" builders—
most dead by now, though some, no doubt, at work
scattered throughout Prague, in little flats, alone—
feel vindicated in their bitterness,
if bitterness survives absurdity.

I'd like to know that once or twice a year
an old man, whose hands are soft from idle thought,
comes, by tram or car, to gaze a while
and simply marvel that the thing still stands.

St. Vitus

In the great gothic cathedral of Prague—
designed, of course, to scare shit out of peasants,
and so parley a huge and abstract doom
into incontrovertible power—
I strolled, nine months after the gentle purge.

A god who dices with the universe
surely will not care for such drab splendor,
but there it stands, dank, crusted with relics,
neither museum nor sanctuary.

The Holy Roman Empire once murmured there,
and Charles IV is kept in the huge cellar;
I bought a ticket and slumped down the steps
with the other tourists, mostly Germans.

Raised in a nation obsessed with beginnings,
I could not stipulate resolution
as the measure of gross identity;
in the foundation of St. Vitus
large, dirty walls of granite shoulder death,
and I imagined kids through the centuries
screwing in the hollow pockets of rock,

sneaking down, wicked, sweet, full of guilt
yet drawn inexorably to the cool places

near the crypts of kings and bishops, as though
passion justifies what passion hastens.

I was so surprised to see a black face
I smiled and nodded as I passed, but you
took this as salutation and wheeled around
and stopped me. Where was I going? When would I
return? What was I doing in Prague? Did I live
in that building? How did I get a flat
in the heart of town? What kind of writer
was I? Did I speak Czech or French or German?
You were little and wiry and well-dressed.
You were a student from West Africa.
All I'd wanted to do was buy some beers
from that funky gypsy joint around the block.
You said you'd wait for me on the corner,
and I could not believe you were still there
when I returned with bottles filling my arms.
You asked if I wanted company, which
at home may have signalled you were gay,
but I am certain that you were not gay,
that you were just a cheerful, lonely fellow
looking to practice one of your several
languages, seeking perspectives on Prague
and all of its marvelous convolutions.
Wasn't it wonderful what was happening?
Had I gone each day to Wenceslas Square?
Did I believe they could ever change back?
Was I familiar with Havel's dramas?
I could barely hold onto all those beers.
I was in a hurry, and you annoyed me.
I was sorry, but I had to go in.

No, I did not need company; a friend
was awaiting my return. She and I
would eat dinner then go out. I was sorry,
very sorry; I wished you well, and you
said maybe another day you'd return
and we could talk, but all I wanted was
to get away from your unrelenting
friendliness, your intolerable goodness
and sincerity, your huge toothsome smile.
But in the foyer I was troubled by your voice,
so put the bottles down, almost shattering one,
and ran back out, but the street was empty
and the sky was wringing out the last few drops
of sunlight, and where there had been shadows
an even sheen from streetlamps now prevailed.
It is not that you were too good for me,
or that a god wears one mask for you and one
for me, but that excess of sweetness seems,
even in the fading midst of hopeful change,
a mortal mystery in such a world as ours.

The Mothers

In Old Town Square
stoic Jǒn Hus and his mangle
of acolytes pose art nouveau,
black-stone emblem of Czech resolve.
But no Bohemian I had met
took seriously the image.
Indeed, Palach notwithstanding,
no noble conflagration
for these sighing people.
No action without irony.

Citizen of a loud country,
nation of manic hope and shrill
despair, I envied Czechs their Svejk,
their implicit affirmation
of all that is unheroic.
"Laughing beasts," a Nazi governor
had called them. I thought them wholly sane.

But the cost of such sanity
seemed trivial, dull, quotidian;
"light laughter on the face, heavy sorrow
in the heart," one poet said,
though by pervasive irony
the equation often got reversed.

So on that day the mothers of Prague
circled Hus with their infants' trams,

the scrawled bright signs of protest,
and the elemental colors of
the canvas trams and mothers' coats,
appeared for all the world like gentle flames.

"Socialism With a Human Face"

Several times those dizzying weeks
I wondered aloud if "socialism
with a human face" was not still more
than the sentiment of Dubcek's
wounded generation. One young Czech laughed.
"Socialism doesn't work. Our lives are proof!"

How could I, fed Adorno and Marcuse
where a fair mind and sunny disposition
may buy the good life unto death,
preach socialism to the best minds
where Lenin had had the final word
on sex and lyric poetry?

They wanted markets, sleek markets,
and membership in Europe's club.
They harkened back to Masaryk's First Republic,
when, before the confiscations,
Bohemia was prosperous and proud.

The days after Martin Smid got martyred
only to reappear beaten but alive,
no one knew that tanks and troops would not roll in.

Obcanske Forum, Havel as its heart,
was coalescing in the chants
of the disenfranchised "masses."

In the streets after rallies, a calm mulling
persisted into night, and the Square flickered
where students kept their vigil. I watched them
gathered close, wrapped in blankets, sipping hot drinks
brought by friends, their faces sweetened
by ten thousand candles, and considered
that their lives will never be so pure again.

After Frank Zappa's Visit to the Castle

One may imagine him saying to Zappa,
"I've been a fan since 'Weasels Rip My Flesh'."
Yet to know he loves his beer and music,
or that years ago he soldered a crazy
Pirandello to his own Bohemian heart,
does not prepare the credulous outsider
for Havel, designer of chic uniforms!

Less than one year out of prison, newly
ascended to the bloodless seat of power,
it seems he looked upon his Color Guard
and was, if not offended, deeply bothered
by the cut and colors of what they wore,
and so sat down with pen and drafting paper
and sketched out how the uniform should drape
the smart, svelt soldier, and in what hues of blue.

Bohemians, Moravians, and Slovaks
have rarely marshalled marshal acumen.
To see them marching on the castle grounds
ceremoniously grave, one might affirm,
though, the prerogative of small nations
to strut absurdly through the rituals
of masculine identity and pride.

There is a quiet courage of irony
which visits the great lovers in a world
antithetical to their dreams of peace,

21

and no matter his crimes, every prisoner
must know his world by walls and uniforms.

It's not unlikely a troop of Sea Scouts
from Bangor, Maine, or Fresno, California
would whip the Czechoslovak Color Guard,
yet what mother of invention would not squeal
to see her boy decked out by a president?

Stepan From a Balcony

As clerkish Nazis got plugged
into ruins of post-war Germany,
so a club of thugs and thieves—
who fancied the state
their exclusive enterprise—
must grease the wheels that turn
the wheels of daily life
in Czechoslovakia.

Still vexing "the people,"
these petty functionaries
stamp the forms that move
the forms from cubical to
cubical in a great false
economy of winks and bribes;
and when their eyes get dreamy,
and when they sigh and stare,
one may imagine
they drift beyond the fictions
of lesser ideologies,
becoming generic angels
full of wishes and good
intentions, so gentle
in their reveries they
are almost innocent,
almost pitiably
silly for their self-
consumption and the glossy
essence of their dreams,
indeed, almost American:
and therefore lovable,

and therefore dangerous
beyond their functions.

From a balcony, Stepan ranted
over a shrieking PA
to the crowd of pissed-off
faces that he, Party boss
of Prague, would not be cowed
by "fifteen year-old children."
"We are not children!"
the crowd chanted back to him,
and stocky, dog-faced Stepan
stuttered to take back his boast:
"Of course I don't mean you! I mean
those students..." But the crowd
wouldn't stop; the chant swelled
from the narrow street and swarmed
over the elegant arc of the city:
"We are not children!"

Vaculik's Garden

Throughout his garden, things edible and not
flourish mingled in benign disorder.
Full-blown blushing roses nod among trees
that bring forth fruit or blooms, and everywhere

within the barbed-wired beige walls there is bounty
beyond order, such profusion of growth,
by design without design, randomly
touched and tended by Ludvik Vaculik.

His feuilletons so vexed authorities
for twenty years they bugged his life and hauled
him in repeatedly, leveled the same
tired charges, posed the same petty questions,

until it became a quaint occasion
for coffee with his interrogators,
a peripheral, recurring obligation
to set one weary smile against another.

Others have testified to brutalities
which by virtue simply of having happened
changed all comely concepts of humanity
to so much fuming compost of "the heart."

In the garden of Ludvik Vaculik
life riots against the strictures of "garden,"
and the endless enterprise of gardening
is a humbling to whatever it requires.

A broad zone from southern Poland
through central-south Moravia
is dying of chemical blight, and no randy hope
of revolutions nor common markets
will make it once more lush and vital.
Eight months after "the people's triumph"
I'd returned to see my child be born.
Swollen to her eighth month, my child's
strong mother hiked with me five k's
to the Polish border, all the while
quizzing: strom . . . kyticka . . . zeleny . . .
Our child, she insisted, will speak Czech,
will have a Czech identity.
She paused often to pluck berries,
and spoke with humor of her parents,
divorced for years, still hunting mushrooms
in the same frail woods outside Prague:
"They live the same lives, do the same things.
One wonders why they separated."
Blight is a matter of degree,
of course, and that ancient forest
of her country was still attractive;
indeed, the sick rains had so thinned it out
it appeared more lovely for all
the delicate angles of fallen trunks,
and for patches of clearing where
stunted shrubs carpeted the ground.

The Stones

(Prague, August 18, 1990)

On the tram with a spattering
of others who'd left early,
I heard the pyrotechnics
signalling finale,
and thought the "Urban Jungle" set
to have been the one true star,
then wondered if middle-age,
now fluttering at my back,
would mean for me the need
of such a gaudy stage on which
to strut and preen. Probably.
But of course I'd settle
for a considerably smaller one,
or, bitterly, no stage at all.

They'd been brilliant and boring,
the audience huge and uncomfortable
in an all-night, fuzzy drizzle.
Yet it was a smashing success;
from the packed field of Strahov
(the Communists' "largest stadium
in the world"), Havel was seen
dancing behind bullet-proof
plastic in the bleachers, and
everyone marveled at the logistical
complexity, how hundreds
had been required to erect

that set, and hundreds more
for security. Everyone,
of course, knew the songs by heart
and, though a bit stiffly
in the chilly rain, executed his
or her part in this new ritual
of commerce and joy.

We creaked a mile or more
along the spangled Vltava
before I noticed the gorgeous
girl across the aisle
was chattering in English.
Maybe sixteen, her clothes
and jewelry were conspicuously
fashionable; she jangled
and glittered as she spoke
to a rumpled Czech girl
of seeing Poison in Frisco
and the Cure in L.A.

She was stunning in profile,
and I shuddered at the childish
sentences spilling from her
woman's body, the self-
referential effervescence
implicit in her speech,
and the sexual power she
possessed but will not comprehend

until it explodes in her face.
I observed at first
with a twinge of desire,
then sentimental tenderness,
but then as the tram
hushed nearer to Charles Bridge—
sparkling two stops away
through hulking shadows
of saints and kings—I looked on
with mild disgust. For I recalled
how seven months earlier
the students of Prague
had reclaimed their lives,
and I recalled their humility
and wit as they faced that miraculous
withering of power. I recalled as well
how gently they controlled the crowds,
then cleaned the broad boulevards
in the winter-morning dark
after the rallies, and how subtly tender
they were towards one another,
even as the moment they empowered
seemed ripe for histrionics.
They marched; they chanted; they laughed;
they took back everything worth having,
yet a vague conception of this girl's life,
in some measure, defined what so many wanted.
She spoke too fast for her Czech aquaintance,
who nonetheless strained
to follow the litany of groups
and the cities they'd enchanted:

Bon Jovi in Phoenix,
INXS in San Diego,
New Kids in Vegas.
And even as I noted the huge
Rolling Stones banner
now visible from the windows,
floodlighted and stretched
across the marble base
where Stalin's statue
once loomed on a hill above the city;
and remembered how the spirit
of this ancient place
had been chastened by its young
(whose dreams are no less corrupted
than those of our own American beauties);
even as I wallowed a moment
in nostalgia, fully aware
that eternal forms blink on
and off at intervals determined
by the same codes clicking and snapping
in all human loins; I knew that
even as the music swells, envelops, thrives,
here and now rock'n'roll is dead.

A Brief History of Your Conception

I recall the commercial for Radio Free Czechoslovakia
when I was ten, residing in public housing in Norfolk,
Virginia. Checkosowhatchamacallit sounded like a
terrible place to live, worse, even, than public housing in
Newport News. The word looked like a disease, and
being behind the "iron curtain" had to resemble being
in an "iron lung."

When I was fifteen I heard on Armed Forces Radio that
Russia had invaded it. My step-father was sweeping
mines off the coast of Vietnam, and I was a pain in the
ass of Sasebo, Japan. Cherry blossoms littered my path
to the bars downtown.

The summer of '89, I met your mother. She was beauti-
ful and funny and very bright. So I contrived to go to
the country whose name looked like a disease, to the
city Russia had quieted. That autumn, I stood in crowds
of people taking themselves just seriously enough.

There are no pure motives except unto death; my
beckoning you forth from ignorance was that I may
pardon myself, but you are more potent than forgive-
ness. The day preceeding the night you were conceived
I passed through a gauntlet of saints, kings and angels
on Charles Bridge; their stone eyes seemed curious or
malicious, and their heroic postures but propaganda for
paradise. Tourist of a gentle revolution, I was as taken
with the dashed-off slogans taped to subway columns as
with such permanent emblems of "national identity."

32

That night, between the sheets of energy and artifice, you were conceived. My darling, my tiny Bohemian, someday we will toss gray Czech bread to the filthy swans of the Vltava, and you will laugh at my bad Czech grammar. Or a thousand sorrows will darken the sky with slow wings, and I will write your name in salt. Ema, the world is enormous. Pity it, and love accordingly.

The Book of Complaints

(for Pavel Srut)

1

I was told that most
establishments kept
a "book of complaints"
for the sour stories
of the poorly served,
the principle being
familiar to patrons
here in the rich West:
the customer is right,
always, and as such
may stride like a god
through a world of aisles,
touching and choosing.
But the "customer"
was, more precisely,
a mere citizen,
a consuming unit
suffering to shuffle
through too many lines
towards barely stocked shelves.
And when she complained
it was to her shoes
as she queued for fruit,
or to the wall by
the kitchen sink as
she emptied of cans

the plastic bag she'd
kept stashed in her purse,
then to the coal-grayed
sky of sumptuous Prague
as she stood at the
window, in autumn,
a righteous restraint
withering within her.

2

I stood among them,
dumb emissary
of good intentions,
and listened to their
chants and studied their
faces; the autumn
sky would turn to ash
each afternoon in
Wenceslas Square as
the bold crowds swelled, and
the peeved old men in
the castle got grimmer.
"Dominika, what
is he saying now?"
I would ask again
and again, and my
patient friend would pause
to translate the blared
complaints of that hour's

representative,
explaining nuance
and brief history.
"Richard, you just don't
know what it's like to
live under such liars,"
she said, applauding
another public
sentiment of rage,
applauding her youth
and "socialism
with a human face"
(at least the idea
if not the practice).

The night that Jakes
shuffled from power,
a fine rain drizzled
and kids piled into
cars and hammered horns
and swished Czech flags, and
the faces on trams,
even of the old,
in that gold light shined
with contentedness;
the Book of Complaints
seemed, for a moment,
closed.

3

    But it is
never finished; it
lengthens after
death as head skin shrinks
and turns to leather.

Dominika, dear
one, beautiful and
bright, everywhere sour
heads, having spent youth
seeking a cure for
fear of death, find in
the death of passion
a bitter solace.
Benevolent, some
would save the whole world
by dint of dry will
from the body's will,
that half-remembered
dance of the fetus
whose dazzling finish
is each body's first
wailing entry in
The Book of Complaints.

The privileging of
mediocrity
is a sin far worse
than the fratricide
it always inspires.
Dull fathers pull long
faces for the young,
who are not amused,
though learning to laugh
with one's whole body
is the first stage of
a ritual killing.

Where, before, people
laughed bitterly and
to themselves, or in
small, muted clutches
sucking cigarettes
and quaffing rich beer,
from mid-November
to mid-December
they laughed openly
and infectiously.
It is wonderful
to hear such laughter;
a revolution
of laughter often
it seemed, and Kafka,
squinting up from his

own Book of Complaints
in a cramped chamber
in a gray heaven,
surely felt the bliss
of vindication.

4

When poor Martin Smid,
the revolution's
martyr for a day—
his purpled, swollen
face a flag of harm—
was thrust on TV
to prove that he lived,
that the Red Beret
had not quite killed him
(as though the thousands
flocking his shrine of
ten thousand candles
might casually scatter
at proof that he lived)
fact withered beneath
the putrid fictions
of twenty-one years,
and though it no doubt
hurt his face to laugh,
one can only hope
Smid saw the noble

purpose of his death,
and smiled.

5

From the Charles Bridge at
night the Castle shines
in golden floodlights
of ambiguous
glory. Bohemians
stroll the quiet dark,
to my eyes passive,
sighingly pliant.
Yet I am humbled
by the memory
of a dour people
opening their lives
to the world and to
themselves, and chanting
the essential truths
inscribed there, in blood.

To the Old Town Square
the tourists will flock
and yawn up stiff-necked
and still beneath the
Astronomical Clock,
waiting for little
carved saints and Jesus

to spin in their slots,
pirouetting robots
chiming the hour.
Each time I return,
a tablet of Czech
dissolving on my tongue,
I'll stand in the Jewish
Cemetery, among
the shuffled, tilting,
gray, smooth, weathered slabs—
Jews buried ten-deep
signified by mounds—
and think of Levi
placing the clay pill
on his golem's tongue.

On most ragged slabs
are pebbles, each speck
a token, a prayer,
a petrified flower
for the laughing dead.

The revelation,
at first, seems simple:
a "state" is only
the page on which one
inscribes her most bitter,
consistent complaints,

a page filled with ire
scribbled in various
hands, signed boldly, or
left anonymous.
We are the mounting
tallies of each our
discontentedness,
and desire, the un-
inscribable, gets
confounded in the
act of complaining.

6

I regard a world
that is beautiful
and rank, and couch what
I see in language
that is palpable
and rude, for nothing
marked in the cool light
of managerial
regard survives its
last bitter affront
to the gaseous sky
or sooty windows,
and my heart's complaints
I mean to survive
unto the sweet eyes
of those I have loved
and would wish to love.

Amid the almost
funny tilting slabs—
that crammed-packed ghetto
of Prague's lost lovers
tilting as a field
of flowers is ruffled
unevenly by
a randy, swirling,
dank, autumnal breeze—
I will bitch a prayer
for Levi's loveless
automaton, and
for each hovering soul
among the muted,
rain-smoothed, pebble-crowned
slate headstones, and bitch
prayers for the new life
of Prague, pristine page
onto which real lives
will be written, one
complaint at a time.

II

Three Dithyrambs

Queen of Diamonds

Female Chorus Leader:

The dreary autumn that I began to bleed,
I dreamed many nights of a gorgeous queen.
Her hair was yellow, her brow translucent,
and her eyes, her eyes were large and aqua-deep.
The nights she loomed beside my bed, her gown
ashimmer with threads as white as diamonds,
it seemed a candle burned beneath her skin.
Each visit, she extended fisted hands.
Sometimes I chose the left one, which always grasped
a dirty piece of string, or razor blade,
but nights I chose the right hand I awoke
before the revelation of its gift.

Male Chorus:

Praise the street lamps sparkling in shattered glass.
Praise weeds that crack cement in vacant lots.
Praise things that scurry in shadowed alleyways.

Female Chorus:

Sometimes at dawn the eastern sky seems bludgeoned,
as though a god had slammed the skull of night
against the farthest, broadest wall of dark.

Female Chorus Leader:

In early spring the dream ceased all at once.
I even tried to will it back, grew sick

45

for sleeplessness and sorrow at the loss.
Was my queen an angel or a phantom?
Would I never know the gift in her right hand?

Female Chorus:

The moon and stars at dawn are washed away
as though a god hosed down his abattoir.

Female Chorus Leader:

Then one blue day that spring I met a girl,
new to the neighborhood and very strange.
Older than I, she had enormous secrets
at which she hinted but would not confess.
I followed after her and always listened.
The boys buzzed around us, ignoring me,
and I observed how regally she brushed
them all aside, and saw she took no joy
in their frenetic fawnings, even as
a perverse squint-eyed smile would mar her face
when one would slink slope-shoulderedly away.
Her beauty was a cave I crouched within
throughout the punishing heat of afternoons.

Male Chorus and Female Chorus:

Praise tender awakenings on summer nights.

Female Chorus Leader:

But then she led me to the river bank
and spread a blanket out beneath the stars
so we could watch men paint the sky with fire.
We lay some distance from the lounging crowd,
whose faces flattened, lifted to the dark
as if to catch some dripping dregs of light.
As first blue blossoms wilted in the sky,
the lagging muffled boom rattled through me,
and she turned her head upon my arm, then moved
her fingertips across my flushing throat,
then down and through the buttons of my blouse.

Male Chorus:

The dazzling lethargy of dying stars,
match-heads dragged slowly on a wall of pitch.

Female Chorus:

Its axis an orthodoxy of the loins,
the language of pleasure eclipses pleasure,
and we are blinded by the aurora ring.

Male Chorus & Female Chorus:

What lover does not stare upon the sky
and shrink it to dimensions of [his] [her] joy?

Male Chorus Leader:

I passed so many little messages,
a look, a smile, a tender salutation.
Such things do not come easily to me.
But she fills my waking and spills through my sleep.
Her quiet sadness seems too delicate,
too much the essence of abstracted souls
haunting foggy, crowded margins of the world.
We're only colleagues in a little office
training a collective, weary eye on all
the petty transgressions of our company.
It is a vagary of self-policing
that the shiest, least aggressive do the job.
We are sheep who monitor the lives of wolves.
Our office, immaculate if impotent,
hums along from day to day, garnering praise
from those whose bloated budgets we ignore.
Three years her presence in my working life
defines the character of my private hours.
We seem so much alike, yet I cannot say
that repelling force which I so often feel.
What charms me utterly yet holds me off?
What is the fabric of her mystery?

Female Chorus Leader:

Of course her sweetness faded with the season.
She moved on, and on, woman to woman,
a legendary lover of all women

in that hushed community of women
into whose numbers she had ushered me.
I took my own fling at promiscuity,
even a boy or two, but that was show.
I turned prettier with age, sensual,
yet even as I grew more worldly-wise
the torment of my adolescent dream
intensified; what did she represent?
What primal mother-love or mother-loathing,
or intricate subconscious braiding of
the two did my dream queen most signify?
And what gross trinket of salvation or doom
did that anima of adolescence hide?

Male Chorus Leader:

I know other women, have pleasure with some,
and do not at all lead a lonely life.
Family, friends, and occasional lovers
fill my private time, or that much of it
I allow for congenial interaction.
But mostly I prefer to be alone,
though since she soaked into my thoughts and dreams
to be alone is one exquisite pain.
I spend half my working time contriving ways
to brush her arm or smell her subtle scent.
She smiles and chats politely, but that is all.
When once I mustered courage to ask her out,
having rehearsed the casual line for weeks,

she begged off with such cool and stilted grace
I backed away shattered and enchanted.
The Xerox copier shuttles and flashes between
her cubicle and mine; the cooler
gurgles intermittently, and all around
us office romances are blossoming.

Female Chorus:

From roofs of any city's highest towers,
one may gaze, at dusk, upon the moving glow
of traffic, and office windows going dark
or burning yellow long into the night.

Male Chorus:

To love as though one's object of affection
were wholly made of stuff not of this world
is such despicable innocence as gods
inflict upon us for their gross amusement,
being themselves the quintessence of our dreams.

Female Chorus:

The violence of the maniac who hurts
for mortal fear of tenderness marks off
parameters of heaven's killing floor.
Let gentle-natured men put on their wings
of paraffin and glide into the sun.
Let the anger of men boil in the fat
of their best and worthiest intentions.

50

Let silly titillation pass no more
for what we need of grave and healing passion.

Female Chorus Leader:

I know he's smitten, hopelessly in love,
though the hopelessness is rough measurement
less of his capacity for loving
than my self-knowledge and intransigence.
I play with him a little, lead him on
in ways so subtle he doesn't even know.
For all the amusement he affords me,
I've actually mustered some affection for him,
affection born of pity for a fool.
Is there nothing more pathetic than a man
chained to an obsessive, unrequited love?
All the power they stake out in courtship
fizzles faced with feminine disinterest.
Yet there is nothing so tender as women
soon after men have hurt them long and deeply.
I have loved two sweethearts thus afflicted,
taken them in and soothed away the hurt.
Both left for other men, further disaster,
but changed a little for what I gave them,
a heightened capacity for disinterest,
I hope, and memories of slow tenderness.
My office puppy, like most any man,
would change into a monster of disinterest.
I've seen such transformations many times.
Hormonal drives, transferred through the lie
that programs every masculine self-presence,

power a cottage industry of love
which fails soon, leaving women unemployed
or indentured to some bottom line of need.
It's all a matter of passion's timing,
how men begin enthralled but then progress
by swift degrees into desolation,
as women, desolate at birth, journey towards
a dream of utter, unabashed enthrallment.

Male Chorus:

Praise the serious words of serious men.
Praise the wholesome tyrant ranting to a crowd.
Praise belligerent saints chanting recipes
for grace to children who are the heart of grace.
Praise politicians when they tally power
tapping dollars on their calculators.
Praise the piercing minds of acerbic wits
compensating for secret, withered lives.
Praise demented heroes of forgotten wars
braying epithets at their radios.
Praise the cop who beats the kid who shot the kid
who sold the drugs that killed the kid who shot
the cop who kicked and beat the kid who sold
the drugs that killed the kid who shot the kid
who knifed the kid who broke his mother's heart.

Female Chorus:

Praise shivering breadths of scattered city lights.
Praise muted voices in a crowded room.

Praise sacred rage of children much abused.
Praise ministers of doom on television.
Praise conspiracies of righteousness.
Praise the distance that a leaf must carry
blown fluttering across a bright autumnal sky.
Praise hands of a woman lifted against the hand
that hangs clenched upon the air above her.

Male Chorus Leader:

The essence of it I know is quite unreal,
unreal as well the urge which is no more
than relentless forces channeled by the vague,
arbitrary rules of sweet engagement.
Even at its gentlest, pursuit of love
so often feels a predatory act.
No doubt my boyish, shy fixation hides
the fierce self-loathing of a man too meek
to alter circumstances of his life.
It is, perhaps, just cowardly diversion.
Yet who does not feel recreated in the flesh
when love's delusions flair upon the brain?
The cultivated lie which first released
the civilizing power of hope for change
tethers still the human will to phantoms.
We who are doomed know we are doomed, yet dance
out on the shimmering brink of destiny,
as though the progress into nothingness
proceeds according to the mandates of
not actuary tables, but fairy tales.

Female Chorus Leader:

That day, I hope when I am very old,
I rasp my final breaths upon the world,
my queen of diamonds, more ravishing
and splendid than my adolescent dreams
could ever have contrived, will turn her wrist
so the delicate veins are visible,
and her fingers will uncurl like tendrils.
I know this as I know a gentle rain
may signify implicit boundaries of
a flower dying towards its loveliest
moment, as though disaster is its own
reward for all living things, sentient or not.

Male Chorus and Female Chorus:

The slow, insistent pull of gentle starlight,
like old friends who guide you from a stool
that you may reel through doors onto the night,
precedes collapse of will and vertigo
of terror, as the final hour expires.

Female Chorus:

By mysterious inversion, in men's dreams
women's naked bodies are emblems of death.

Male Chorus Leader:

I am one thing in pursuit, quite another
when I've achieved what I pursued, yet all
the sweetness promised by the fantasy
prepares a lover's palate for a taste
of something only precincts of heaven
may concoct, and to know this is a torment.

Female Chorus and Male Chorus:

Yet as a form of play distracting from
the needs and thoughts which sanctify denial,
the game of Sex and Death is always lost
by virtue of a quick repatriation
of flames to Republics of the Sun,
as passion recalled, in desolate fields
of passion spent, is daylight flashing on
great banked and sparkling rifts of virgin snow.

Eat What You Kill

Female Chorus Leader:

He touched me as he would something precious.

Female Chorus:

When I go to market,
when I shop for meat...

Female Chorus Leader:

The hidden cargo of his private voice
was a preternatural contraband.

Female Chorus:

When I go to market,
when I shop for meat...

Female Chorus Leader:

He made me feel like a special lover.

Female Chorus:

When I go to market,
when I shop for meat,
I squeeze the packages
of creamy bone and tender flesh,
and delight in my purchasing power.

56

Female Chorus Leader:

But when the heart-shaped catalpa leaves
crisped and fluttered down, he grew secretive,
violent, abstract in his moods, and I wept.

Female Chorus:

Among the clean, delicious aisles of market,
where saccharine music numbs the air, I move
from thing to geometric stack of things,
touching and choosing, touching and choosing.

Female Chorus Leader:

He changed so suddenly, he seemed enchanted,
and I, his talisman of ridicule,
became as well the cross he slouched upon
in cathedrals of his waning passion.

Female Chorus:

Produce, canned goods, dairy, deli, frozen things.

Female Chorus Leader:

Then the long sorrow, alone and quiet,
memory like the sewing box my mother
rustled through, untangling the delicate threads.
No woman loves her mother more than when
a man has lied and lied, then disappeared.

Female Chorus:

Fresh salmon, the color of a falling sun,
plumbs the hue of hard love's purple bruises,
rich mounds of liver a bovine pudding...

Female Chorus Leader:

For weeks I lived on air and good intentions,
lounging in chambers of exquisite hunger,
phone unplugged, the television flickering.

Female Chorus:

In the supermarket, death is pretty,
sliced precisely and wrapped in cellophane.

Male Chorus Leader:

In a bar somewhere, I think in Texas,
I fixed upon a neon sign, flashing red,
in which a man riding a bucking bronco
jolted up and off again and again.
For the sake of argument, I'll call the horse
a biological imperative,
the cowboy just another fool in love.

Male Chorus:

Yippi-yi-ay, another roll in the hay!

Male Chorus Leader:

In the great deserts, nothing is wasted.
I've seen black birds hunched over black carrion
and thought from a distance it looked like love.

Male Chorus:

Yippi-yi-ay, another roll in the hay!

Female Chorus:

When I go to market,
when I shop for meat . . .

Male Chorus Leader:

Desert nights, something sticks a tongue in my brain,
and for an hour I am passion's prophet.

Male Chorus:

Yippi-yi-ay, another roll in the hay!

Female Chorus Leader:

I have toyed with the notion of difference.
I mean, once, on a summer veranda,
I let a boy touch me everywhere, but laughed
when his earnest gropings turned to tickles.
Then I marvelled how his face colored rose

59

in the half-light and contorted with shame
for having bungled the chore of arousal.

Male Chorus:

Yippi-yi-ay, another roll in the hay!

Female Chorus Leader:

Yet at some early moment love, the word,
began to simmer at the crowded margins
of each loquacious day, and I could not think
myself a woman but that I would be loved.

Female Chorus:

Through spaces for legs in each silver cart,
from the child's seat that folds down, the loose fruit drops
to linoleum and rolls down the aisle.

Male Chorus Leader:

Between the word and the meat, the mouldering breath
and the apparatus of its shaping,
swoops and glides the carrion will of sex.

Female Chorus:

I have always hated that little seat
in supermarket baskets, not because
I hate the thing for which it was designed,

but for the absence I'm reminded of
as I pile sweet delicacies upon it.

Male Chorus:

I laugh and piss off the brink of disaster.

Female Chorus Leader:

When I'd grown so hungry I could barely move . . .

Male Chorus:

I laugh and piss off the brink of disaster.

Female Chorus Leader:

When I was sure I'd starved the thing within me . . .

Male Chorus:

I eat what I kill in the wilderness.

Female Chorus:

When I go to market,
when I shop for meat . . .

Female Chorus Leader:

When it had seemed to cease to move within me . . .

Male Chorus Leader:

Ten East from Houston, five AM, the dark
spring sky commences a gradual blossoming.
The bayou masses gray on either side
of a six-lane interstate ruled by trucks.

Female Chorus Leader:

When it had seemed to cease to move within . . .

Male Chorus:

Trucks hauling chemicals, perishable things,
trucks packed with produce, canned goods and meat.

Male Chorus Leader:

In Euripides' *Bacchae*, the brash young king
angers the fey god of vegetation,
and who doesn't get a little misty-eyed
when Mother wakens from her reverie
and stares upon the severed head of love?

Female Chorus Leader:

I joked of eating for two, and all that first
trimester assumed its purblind every need.
But then his pretty words stopped feeding me.
Romance rotted in his eyes and on his tongue
and he philosophized my joy away.

62

Why could he not recall the promises
implicit in attentive strokes and glances?
Had I become a monster with two heads?
I had become a monster with two heads,
one weeping constantly, one sequestered in
a tangled nest of roots below my heart.

Male Chorus:

A formal, rank occasion for tender pain,
all courtship is a manufactured bliss.
Contrived caresses fix rapacious will,
and all we coo or whisper is a lie.

Female Chorus:

Squatting in the gloom or by a flame,
the squalls and moans of children all around,
the women of the clan await their men
and yearn for bloody meat they may bring back.
The moon is round and high upon a hill
and things that thrive in darkness howl and click.
One woman grinds dried roots between two stones.
One rocks a dying child before the fire.
One chews a leaf that makes her numb, then dreams
of men who shuffle, chanting, shouldering high
great dripping shanks of red and marbled flesh.

Male Chorus Leader:

As broken lines of causeways stuttered by,

I found a clarity on which my guilt
could stand and castigate my grimmer motives.
I gave her all, then took it back, and fled.

Female Chorus Leader:

The earliest stories of what we are
show gods as well as mortals eating children.
I lay before my open bedroom window,
breathing at the rhythm of the soothing breeze,
too weak to move, and wondering if there were
a mechanism by which absorption of
that fetted fist of protein might sustain me.
Such speculation was delirium,
and soon ejection of the thing grown foreign
in death proceeded, and I lay in blood
until a woman friend, guessing my state,
spied thing and me linked as though in carnage,
and jerked my back to weep among the living.
I cannot say the drug of his affection,
taken suddenly away, caused sickness of
an unremittingly convulsive loss.
Withdrawl of affection sucks nothing away,
yet absence of that absence is profound,
and such profundity consumes the will.
I've no idea what I wanted from his love
beyond an affirmation of my life,
one best achieved by work or meditation.
I played the fool, and knew myself a fool
to lay my passions bare before a man.

64

Male Chorus Leader:

Who is more culpable in passion's lie,
he in blind pursuit who perpetrates it,
or she who thrives upon mendacity?

Male Chorus and Female Chorus:

In the glimmering aisles, all the jars and boxes
vie for our affection, whispering lies,
exaggerating capabilities,
listing all their odious components
in the smallest, least conspicuous print.
Being thus romanced, our thoughts of death subside,
until we reach the rows of packaged meat,
and etherizing Muzak turns grotesque
as artificial air grows rank and chill.

Male Chorus Leader:

Vaguely repentant, even ashamed, I lunged
from one false enthrallment to another,
my affection like a blight of locusts,
though more voracious, quiet, and complete.
Yet when she starved herself to kill the child,
then reported the deed as liberation,
I did not know who or what was free of what
or whom, and cried alone in voiceless dread.

Female Chorus Leader:

When I was sure the thing was dead within,
that I myself was but a rasping tomb . . .

Male Chorus Leader:

The spine-whittling Doppler whoosh of trucks
rumbling west, racing a flashing dawn . . .

Male Chorus:

Praise God of light and limitless spaces.
Praise God of darkness and emploding stars.
Praise God of words and their vast dominion.

Female Chorus:

My wrath pursues its tail in a dark field.
Yet I may not wander on a moonless night.
Alone in open spaces, I am prey.

Male Chorus:

Praise God the hunter in the field of light.
Praise His stealth and patience among the stars.
Praise His true transparent eye and perfect aim.

Female Chorus:

I did not explode from my father's brow,

66

but was constituted from a pool of blood,
and remain, in essence, a pool of blood.

Female Chorus Leader:

When I told him on the phone the thing was dead,
a quavering buzz of traffic framed his silence,
and I could only pity him his silence.

Male Chorus:

And the brutal father tore half-formed flesh
from the new charred corpse of its foolish mother,
then slashed his thigh and stashed the thing inside.

Female Chorus:

Who does not reckon a fruitful woman
the measure of renewal and abundance?
What more fecund image than a woman fat
with life cruising gleaming aisles of market?

Male Chorus:

How passion's carnal play gets reconciled
with passion's grim directive will define
the gross aesthetic value of our lives
when shelter, food, and leisure are sufficient.

Female Chorus Leader:

I am innocent, yet wholly culpable,
and offer no apology or excuse
for self-denial that siphoned another life.
It was my legal right to purge myself.
The termination was not violent,
was not achieved by artificial means.
The thing began as passionate affection;
an assumption of good faith marshalled it
from that crowded zone of nothingness and bliss.
But tenderness recalled became a hell,
and I, alone yet not alone, contained
the literal essence of a bloody lie.

Male Chorus Leader:

Who can stare upon the sky, night or day,
and not desire to fill the immensity?
I have felt such terror beneath that dome
my hands have trembled and my eyes moistened.
Consider how each star is self-consuming,
how even that rage eight minutes away
is slowly starving towards a grand dispersion.
Shall I now mourn the lolling cinder earth
will be, the inevitable extinction?
I should rather wash my face and change my shirt,
keep my line of vision taut and level,

and move out upon the boulevards of light.
There is much transitory sweetness there.

Female Chorus Leader:

I cock the night and hold it to my brain.
I shall remain utterly amazed, or sleep.

Brother Love

Chorus:

The fibrillations of a man's sorrow,
brief consequence of terror in self-knowledge,
presage a bottomless plunge towards solitude.
Perhaps he cries for all the pain he's caused.
Perhaps he curls up in the dark and sobs.
Perhaps he presses death between his eyes
and squeezes off his one unselfish act.
But each lucky man has one brother in pain,
his life lived otherwise, or parallel.

Gay brother:

I have done one terrible thing. I was born.
I have performed one great act many times.

Straight brother:

To think the same woman gave breath to us,
the same man coaxed us from the permutations
of his marvelous body's difficult code.

Gay brother:

In those woods behind our uncle's house
a path as narrow as a boy's quick stride
burned serpentine through brush to the black stream.

Chorus:

Praise innocent journeys on summer days.

Gay brother:

By the fallen enormous trunk of oak
that breached the breadth of the small water's flow,
I found a dirty piece of cloth, some boy's
shed briefs he'd tossed aside before plunging in.

Chorus:

Praise sweet guilt of confused awakenings.

Straight brother:

I think I knew his body's revelation.
I think I knew the day he found his path.

Gay brother:

I plucked it up, and brushed it off, and held
it to my cheek, and felt a sobbing rage
rush through my groin, and realized friendship meant
to me a thing, an act, a symmetry
that other boys would fear and wish to kill.

Straight brother:

Fraternal twins, our raw coterminous fates

71

distinct at birth yet mutually determined,
we grew into an intimate self-loathing
indicative of primal brother love.

Chorus:

At inception, God the baby wept and wailed
to conjure forth a flash and silver surface,
and seeing that It was a lovely God,
cooed itself a sphere of machinations,
of whirling contradictions signifying
each to each the essence of necessity.

Straight brother:

We lay in separate beds and whispered dreams
and lies and boasted, like our father did,
that we would have the world for ransoming.
He was my passionate foe and confidant.
When we touched, it was for brutal pleasure,
wrestling on the fragrant morning grass.

Chorus:

Praise the angular beauty of the day.
Praise the frank inconstant stars and summer skies.
Praise the stiffening contours of the night.

Straight brother:

But then it seemed a sentimental pall

72

of adolescent doom covered him in smoke,
and he stepped forth another than I had known.
He read of chivalric lives—always soft,
fair and verdant—idyllic nobility,
as though on the plane of fictions and dreams,
where nothing shits nor flies insult the air,
his rooting, squealing new desire might sleep.
I did not have the heart for what he was,
and just the faintest concept of the laws
of nature his abominations cursed.
Several humid nights I followed him to town
and observed him lounging on a gaslit stoop
until a fatherly car would slow, open,
and brother of my flesh would pause, then enter.
Shocked, unfamiliar with the symptoms of grief,
I strangled soft affection for his name.

Chorus:

He who awakens to his mortal difference,
he who is changed and suffers change, will plunge
into Death's tangled currents and emerge
gasping, dripping mortality, coughing prayers.

Gay brother:

First I was darling of the dirty secrets,
the cloistered fancy of the timid butch.
"Just think of me as your special daddy,"
one pink-skinned, balding Volvo told me.
Later, I found a crayon on the seat

in back, and slipped it in my pocket with
the bills he slipped me before he sped away.
But I wanted love, not old men's money.
I wanted a special friend, like a brother,
only more intimate, rough yet tender.

Chorus:

The burning issues on the tongues of angels
are heaven's forfeitures of reasoned mercy.
When God pontificates, the speed of light
is that at which the throngs of blessed ones pass
from bliss to boredom, to nodding somnolence.

Gay brother:

Romantic, pale, hazed light of surrender,
the whole round thing stopped the night like a cork.
A starry effervescence seemed to hiss
with joy I heard but could not see, face-down
as I was in grass, my lover's fingers wound
through my hair as though I galloped in the dark.

Straight brother:

I gazed over the rim of a stinking can,
not twenty yards from where a writhing flower
shed violent silhouettes across the brink
of shrubs and stones that lined the river bank.
What churning pain was this that he called love?
What rank humiliation drove his needs?

Persecution halted with terminal grunts.
The agent of pain backed out like a cat,
drew up the denim gathered at his ankles,
sniffed and smirked at the indolent moon, then strolled
towards spangled city streets, smoothing his hair.
My brother lifted to his elbows, then knees,
his face pouring down like a snapped blossom.

Chorus:

Deep zones of mystery are passing away.
Great healing jungles are aching with flames.
The waters are choking. Skies dissipate.
Who, seeking love, should wish procreation?

Straight brother:

He beat us for the sake of filial love,
a father's proud desire that sons should be
the living monuments of how he lived.
There was of course a ritual to it all.
Feeling left his face like draining liquid,
and he stood as still as God the longest moment,
until he slowly pointed to the hook
where his razor strap would droop like bacon.
The offender's part was to fetch it to him
then lay across the couch arm, mute supplicant,
pants down. But he would sometimes make us wait.
Often a sweaty minute, one time with me
an hour before he lashed my flesh five times
ferociously. The pain would burn for days.

But once, I don't know why, my brother
lay bare-assed across the couch arm for an hour,
then another, until the house grew dark
and still he did not move nor father come
to lash him for some boyish indiscretion.
That morning I awakened to his weeping,
and when I peered across the banister
I saw him still arched over, fouled and wet,
sobbing for forgiveness, begging for pain.

Chorus:

When angels mourn, the lamps grow dim in nurseries,
and newborns paw the air and cast blurred eyes
upon dark ceilings, where the new dead float.
The infants, whose brief souls are angel's tears,
are so pristine the blessed can but weep the more,
though new dead grumble for a quick revenge
on those who weep to weep that perfect soul
whose nature is the slide to such corruption
as they, being dead, escaped yet yearn for still.

Gay brother:

That world I found within the world was true
to those shrill longings chanting in my blood.
When acrimony of my father's voice
intensified beyond what I could bear,
when the world outside my world had choked with shame
for what by nature, or unnatural design—
the difference to my heart is only words—

76

my body's separate will had shunned convention,
I orphaned my soul, speculation's breath,
unto the living city's lap of danger,
where no mother's sighs, father's rage, brother's shock
could burst exquisite dreams of satisfaction.

Chorus:

Praise the blank wall where many families weep
a sorrow greater than the world's blue turning.
Praise the falling fist and the flenching brow.

Straight brother:

These twenty years since I twice saw him so,
deranged and glowing with humility,
my righteousness has softened for the wisdom
that I have since curled over for a few
no less inglorious humiliations,
and if he remains a mortal mystery to
me still, I am puzzled with affection.
He lay now, rasping breaths, punk to a system
more concerned with bed space than with healing.
Is there a less ennobling sphere of passage
than this dull chrome and linen house of numbness?
White smocks pass through; like me they only wait.
I do not blame them for their helplessness,
though their officious posturing revolts.
Gloved, the attendants turn him gingerly
and adjust the hissing nozzle in his mouth.
Ashen, diminished-to-bone, unconscious thing,

he seems a hatchling fallen from its nest.
I would cup it in my hands, and running
to the house shout, "Mother! Look what I have found!"

Chorus:

Praise brief horror which is the death of dying.

Straight brother:

But she would not be there, nor anyone else,
only he as a small boy, reading his book.
He would stare into my hands, then look up
and smile a worried smile into my eyes.
Together we would fashion a cotton nest
and keep it, a day or two, between our beds.

✌ III

On the first cool day in half a year,
an October Sunday in New Orleans,
I waken happy in my new house.
You know, sunlight, breezes, bells,
coffee, thick newspaper, all that.
When I shuffle out to walk my little dog
there's a kid, fourteen maybe,
staring down and holding his dark face
in his dark hands, on the stoop
of the abandoned house next door.
His shoes are torn and cruddy;
his filthy shirt is blooming
from his back pocket; his bony torso
is ashy black and sunken. Why do I think
in childhood he wept violently and often,
that he'll spend his adolescence
constructing alternatives to weeping,
just one of which is to sit alone
in breezy morning sunlight
and dream himself beyond the dull,
fixed circumstances of his life?
My brain is glossy with the world's news,
my heart aglow with sugar and caffeine.
all over town citizens are praying or plotting,
sleeping late or taking stock.
He looks at me and mumbles he's just resting,
which means don't worry, White Bread,
I won't smash your Ford or rape your dog
or steal your VCR, just don't worry.
Drag your silly puff around the block
and disappear. Today, this hour,

I am meant for this stoop. This air
I breathe is mine all mine, this sunlight
and sputter of tiny breezes just for me.
I'm hungry, but that's okay, for now.
For now, we are quiet in the flat regard
with which we hold each other; he drops his head
once more and I walk on, recalling hunger,
the unspeakable passions it engenders,
the ugly, useless wisdom of it.
With tainted sadness I remember such
as all the elegant systems
I've since peered upon will never steel
against the acid fact of physical despair,
but when I turn and trot my little love
back home to face the kid again, to speak
to him not like a father, but to ask
him into my house to eat, he is blocks away.

Black English

How to say the distance, not the difference,
is the problem.
In her Freshman composition
Shellanda writes that most men
treat cars better than they treat women,
describes her brother rubbing
wax for hours
into red-washed steel and blinding chrome;

she is hilarious and tactful implying
the absurdity of his erotic care, and suggesting
he loves women only in his dreams.

I imagine Shellanda's brother cruising
St. Charles on a Friday night, easing
his bright machine past the homes of wealthy whites.
There is no bitterness in his face, no wonder,
only the self-satisfaction of a young man
who keeps what he owns looking nice.

Maybe at home he's one mean bastard.
But on the rich strip at night just driving
and looking around, listening to loud
music and not judging, not judging
even himself, he feels the TV
in his brain click off when the soft

white of a trolly's headlamp—
blocks away—seems a false though lovely
offering for which words will not do,

and do not matter.

A Ride

The young one is cheerful and kind.
The spread fingers of his hand are gentle
as they guide my head to miss the door frame.
He tells how I may sit comfortably
with my sore knuckles behind me,
speaks calmly and frankly about my chances
of getting out by morning.
On the way to the station,
we converse through the silver vents
that line the plexiglass shield.
The one who drives is distracted and weary;
at a stop he turns his wedding band,
stares over his shades at the three-tiered lights,
whistles three wretched bars of a dead melody.
The young one is younger than I,
inarticulate, eager, tethered firmly to the material world.
I think, in the midst of our chatter,
that there is no reason why he should not love his gun.
He asks what I do and I tell him I write.
From that moment,
he speaks with excitement he tries to conceal.
In three or four minutes
he narrates several dangerous police adventures.
The driver is lost in thought.
I get the feeling the young one
would like to know me better,
maybe be my friend.
He does not know, as the other does,
that I loathe him with my soul,
which does not exist
except at times like this.

These New Angels

These new angels are different, quite different.
One sees them gathered in packs of five or seven
in semi-circles, bouncing on haunches,
phosphorescent in their nakedness,
pecking bits of flesh from roadkills,
or playing a game with marked stones
similar to dice, but more complex.

They are the new idle rich,
or swell heaven's dole.
Either way, they don't pay taxes.

Therefore, I, nervous agnostic
vexed utterly by what I cannot know,
pray mechanically for their swift repatriation,
and write terse letters to my congresswoman.

Lafitte

After one has been dead a long time,
the life he left gets conflated with others;
then, drifting through changes, noting a few,
a soul may feel time as a body sweet
fever coming on on a chilly night,
and so, if I did not live adventures
of that rogue Lafitte, they adhere like the smell
of dirty smoke to essential fabric
of what I am and may presume to be.
When I stoop to haunt, I am Lafitte.

I blow above the corrugated tiles
and through the iron black lace work of Vieux Carre,
gleaning quaint passions of the living,
those plush, adorable sensations they take
for ecstasy. Indeed, until one has died,
until one has felt the light crack, then crumble
and spill forth the fury of negation,
until one has been thereby anointed,
warm secretions and mutual frictions
are the pitiful measure of "transcendence."
Each death is a forever fuck, a passion
beyond corporeal head or heart, without
pretence of romance or "need" of anyone;
it is lived life in all its particulars
we the dead can't stop fucking, for to cease
is to uncouple sentience from wonder,
and that's the fabled hell of gross self-knowledge.
I, Lafitte the blacksmith and storied rogue,

therefore bear exquisite witness, and am charged
with ushering from their terror—through the lives
of those who killed them—all the slaughtered ones
in this sector of the river's city.
That is, each victim may observe his own
passing and know the shrill joy of his killer,
feel the reciprocity of murder,
when that thief of his breath flees the dark market
of his cooling flesh, to burn on the night
like a television gnawing shadows.
And as I speak upon the nerves of this
scribbler, this "poet," this wedge of pregnant cloth,
even as he bellows forth, puffed with my
fancy, rudderless but that I should rock
the swells, I, the dead pirate Jean Lafitte
am drawn to a crime as by a rich galleon.

The street shimmers in pale gas light, and where
a pinched strip of Burgundy intersects
with Ursuline, an intermittent patch
of jutting angles, shadows and flickerings,
is occupied by one resolved to kill.
The footfall thickens, and the predator's heart
blurs like gasping wings in an airless jar.
I pause to savor his adrenaline rush,
and even as the traffic on Rampart Street
seems a steady drizzle after midnight,
a battered cab glides through intersections
with a herd of drag queens for the strip joints
up on Bourbon, and the boy with a gun

and a need and an anger bangs his back
against the radiating bricks, freezes,
until the car is past and a quick glance
to all points confirms that no one is near,
no one but the mark, the pale idiot
whose money might as well be boiling cabbage
it so stinks the air before him as he strides.

A savage blossoming of human wills
records back, through separate blood lines, until
converging on the festered origin
of tragical necessity and terror;
and all the trapped and useless dead applaud
within the civic theatre of nothing.
I give the victim his moment inside
the killer, the vision of his own demise,
and let him feel the rush of stripping his
shocked self-becoming-corpse of gold watch, gold
chain and tie clasp, thick wallet and shoes.
Then I let him drift among the stars awhile.
Then I let him find his place among the dead.

I, the rogue, blacksmith, pirate Jean Lafitte,
or someone like him, or someone who loved
someone like him, and was hurt unto death.

Perhaps I was a woman or a boy

jilted by the cad, one who wore his shirt
to bed and wept until the sleeves were soggy.

Always, the torment of identity,
and the curious perspectives love affords . . .
There is no God, and He is merciful.

Cold Front

(for Michael Mooney)

Out there, in a real wind
doing noises that have
been variously described,
my itinerant soul,
sour function of my breath,
scavenges among words
affixed to dying things.
Out there, Samuel Beckett is God,
my soul His puppet . . .
my soul which a hired lover
might slip over her hand
to make a nervous client smile,
before wrapping his little beast
in its red-felt mouth.
Out there, the wind is a hired lover
wrapping all things,
even Sam Beckett, who,
for my purposes tonight,
is the old sick guy on Saint Louis Street
who never begs for money
but who seems to do okay, anyway,
for a dying alcoholic.
Out there, God is compelling my soul
to stroke the faces of buildings
and rub the contours of parked cars,
to make the lids of trash cans quiver
and scraps of paper brush over the cool cement.
Out there, Sammy Beckett

has a few choice words for the college boys
who taunt Him and spit beer in His face.
The neatly-dressed little pricks
don't know who they're messing with.
My God is an angry God,
my soul the wind.

Eating the Kennedys

It's ironic that famine brought them here,
for I'd say, "President Kennedy!"
and my hunger shriveled.
I would not have to go to the corner store
and steal a Mars bar,
nor would I have to swipe pieces of food
from my siblings' hands.
We were often hungry
in a neighborhood of hunger,
a square half-mile of boring angles of brick
at the farthest reaches of the New Frontier.
But a Kennedy was president,
swimming courageously over our heads,
and his whole huge family swam behind him,
the children dog-paddling or riding
their mothers' backs,
and we, the entire nation,
rich and poor, black and white and other,
rose from the darkest depths
and ripped and tore at them,

or on Sundays, even after the slaughter in Dallas,
we'd make a ritual of it;
whole neighborhoods bellied up
to huge aluminum vats.

The joyous slurping and swilling
of millions eating great dripping
handfuls of Kennedy is a sound
for which I shall always feel nostalgia.

95

The Surfer

"Father, you needn't punish me anymore.
I shall punish myself now."
> — Freud

Cold April ocean thrilled the surfer's skin
And shocked his brain alert; graphing the flow,
The first full minute after he'd sliced in,
Undulating upon the drift below
The shifting drifts of salty morning air,
He (serpentine) stared out at the charmed swells,
Forgot mere physics of how they could tear
White dripping roots that blurred to green then fell
To curling spread of aqua-smooth release.
That storied movement was destination.
Like one issued grim orders to police
A turbulent range defining nations,
Between the gray, brake-boulders at his lee
And a thin, sweeping sand bar, he shuttled
Parallel, as grieving to memory.
Sensation palpable as passion pulled
A part of him passion was not meant to reach,
The quiet, dry center where balance gripped
His spine, grapnelled his will onto the beach.
A buoy frigged upon the line where currents ripped
A quarter mile beyond where breakers rise.
He'd seen a tourist paddle out that far
To dumb-show for a lover, then heard the cries,
High rasps of terror diminished in air
Weighted with the ocean's contrabass.
Sex and dancing define repetition

In lyric terms of mirroring and pace.
This is what he does, what must be done,
When doing must be felt so he may feel.
Others waken to their dread and live it;
Dreading life, he wakens squatting in the peel
Of water pushing water to a limit
His mother voiced in pain when he was born.
His longest ride he always dreams his last.
Young men look back upon themselves and mourn
Futures in repetitions that are past.

Notes

I hope it doesn't rankle that the poems in the first section are not arranged chronologically, though they do indeed chronicl three stays in Czechoslovakia over a twelve-month period: the first from early September to mid-October of 1989, the second from early November to mid-December, the third from early June to the end of August, 1990. I witnessed, therefore, that complex society, whose cultural history is rich and varied, transform suddenly yet with comparative gentleness from a police state into a pluralistic democracy. I also witness the birth of my only child, Ema, in Prague to her Czech mother on August 29.

"The Mothers"

Jón Hus was the Bohemian religious rerformer burned as a heretic in 1415.

Jan Palach set himself on fire in January of '69 to protest the Soviet invasion.

Svejk, of course, is The Good Soldier Svejk.

"Socialism With a Human Face"

Dubcek was the political leader of Czechoslovakia during the "Prague Spring" of 1968, and coined, or at least popularized, the phrase "Socialism with a human face." He was brought down, with the rest of his reformist government, by the subsequent Soviet invasion. He was recently leader of the country's parliament, a largely ceremonial role.

Martin Smid, a university math student, was thought to have been killed in the November confrontation between students and riot police. It is no exaggeration to say that his martyrdom, brief though it was, hastened the "Velvet Revolution." Inasmuch as the demonstration had been in honor of the memory of Jan Opletal, a student who had been shot by the Nazis exactly fifty years earlier, Smid immediately became mythically linked with him as well as with

Palach, who coincidentally had publicly burned himself to death some twenty years earlier, shortly after the Soviet invasion. The day after the student confrontation with police, the entire city rallied in outraged solidarity with the students. Within a couple of days, two Martin Smid math students were propped before television cameras, the first in color, the second, badly beaten, in black and white. But by then it didn't matter that Smid hadn't been killed. He'd been a martyr just long enough to get the rest of the population behind the students, for the daily rallies in Wenceslas Square had begun.

"After Frank Zappa's Visit to the Castle"

Zappa was enthusiastically welcomed to the castle by President Havel in the early summer of '90. With all the media coverage of a state visit. Havel, indeed, redesigned the uniform of his color guard. It should be remembered that Havel had gotten out of prison less than a year before being elected president.

"Stepan From His Balcony"

In a speech from the balcony of Obcanske Forum in July of 1990, Havel railed against Communist functionaries, still necessarily in positions of practical authority, who were not only slowing infrastructural reforms, but in fact were still skimming huge sums of money from federal coffers. Stepan was the Party boss of Prague, and ordered the attack on the students. He is now in prison.

"Vaculik's Garden"

I had the honor of conducting an interview with Ludvik Vaculik in July of '90. He is, after Havel, arguably the country's most beloved and respected formerly-dissident writer. I knew his work from the English translation of *A Cup of Coffee With My Interrogator*. His *Czech Dream Book* will soon be out in English. My interview with him, along with translations of two of his feuilletons written since the revolution, appeared in the Summer, 1991 number of *New England Review*.

"The Book of Complaints"

is dedicated to Pavel Srut, one of the sweetest men and finest lyric poets of his generation. A good friend of Havel, he refused to publish his own work as long as writers such as Havel and Vaculik were officially forbidden to publish.

Milos Jakes was the decrepid, by most accounts shrewd though inarticulate and stupid, General Secretary of the Communist Party.

"Levi's loveless automaton" is, of course, the first robot (a Czech word). As legend has it, the great Rabbi Levi (Lowy) activated his creation by either placing a clay tablet or, by another account, a piece of parchment with a prayer written on it, in the creature's mouth.

Three Dithyrambs

No one really knows how the most ancient dithyrambs manifested as performances or as texts. Inasmuch as Greek tragedy is thought at least in part to have evolved out of this choral lyric form, I simply tried to imagine backwards, as it were, from Aeschylus. It is my unschooled intuition that the fragments of ancient dithyrambs we do have bear little resemblance to those performed by, say, Arion and his troop.